M.V.P.
Most Valuable Player

Eric Lindros

Chris W. Sehnert

Published by Abdo & Daughters, 4940 Viking Drive, Suite 622, Edina, Minnesota 55435.

Copyright © 1996 by Abdo Consulting Group, Inc., Pentagon Tower, P.O. Box 36036, Minneapolis, Minnesota 55435 USA. International copyrights reserved in all countries. No part of this book may be reproduced in any form without written permission from the publisher.

Printed in the United States.

Cover Photo credit: Allsport Photos
Interior Photo credits: Wide World Photos, pages 12, 15, 16, 19, 23, 26, 28
Bettmann Photos, pages 5, 7, 8, 11

Edited by Paul Joseph

Library of Congress Cataloging-in-Publication Data

Sehnert, Chris W.
  Eric Lindros /Chris W. Sehnert
  p. cm. -- (MVP)
  Includes index
Summary: Profiles the life and career of a Canadian-born hockey player who is one of the youngest winners of the MVP award.
ISBN 1-56239-545-9
1. Lindros, Eric, 1963- --Juvenile literature. 2. Hockeyl players--Canada--Biography--Juvenile literature. [1. Lindros, Eric. 2. Hockey players.] I. Title. II Series: M.V.P. most valuable player.
GV848.5 L56S45 1996
796.962'092--dc20
[B]   95-45628
                                                          CIP
                                                           AC

Contents

ONE OF A KIND

Once in a great while, a hockey player comes along who is head and shoulders above the rest. A player whose unique talents can be recognized when they are very young. Someone with the ability to turn an ordinary hockey team into a champion.

In the 1960s, Bobby Orr of the Boston Bruins skated with an intensity that had never been seen before. Wayne Gretzky came to the National Hockey League (NHL) in 1979, and began to rewrite the record books. Mario Lemieux was the next player to change the course of NHL history, leading his Pittsburgh Penguins to Stanley Cup championships in 1991 and 1992.

As the sport of hockey heads into the 21st century, another standout performer seems destined to carry the torch of greatness. He is the Philadelphia Flyers' center, Eric Lindros. At the age of 22, he won the NHL's Most Valuable Player Award. His climb to the top has been marred with controversies, but his destination has remained clear.

Eric Lindros tries on his new Philadelphia Flyers jersey, 1992.

CENTER OF ATTENTION

Eric Lindros was born February 28, 1973, in London, Ontario, Canada. His family moved to Toronto when he was 10 years old.

Eric's parents, Bonnie and Carl Lindros, have done much to help him achieve the level of success he has enjoyed. Bonnie is a nurse, and Carl worked as an accountant before taking over as Eric's business manager. Both were talented athletes. Bonnie ran track and field in high school. Carl was drafted by Edmonton of the Canadian Football League, and played minor league hockey for the Chicago Blackhawks organization.

Eric is the oldest of three children in the Lindros family. He has one brother, Brett, and one sister, Robin. As a young boy, Eric was full of energy. He could ride a bicycle without training wheels by the age of three. His father built an ice rink in their backyard to keep Eric busy during the winter. Soon after, he was playing hockey in a neighborhood league.

Hockey became an obsession for young Eric. He loved to put on his hockey equipment even if it was just to ride his bike around the neighborhood.

Toronto's skyline reflects off Lake Ontario.

Number one NHL draft pick Eric Lindros (right) is congratulated by his mother (left) after he is named by the Quebec Nordiques as their first-round choice. In the center is Eric's brother, Brett.

By the time Eric was nine years old, his mother began to realize he was a special athlete. He was clearly better than the other players his age.

Eric made hockey his top priority. He played trumpet in his school band, but the demands of the sport caused him to give up the instrument. He didn't have a lot of friends growing up because he was always busy on the ice. At the age of 13, he was practicing with the 15- and 16-year-old kids on St. Michael's College Junior-B team, near Toronto.

The coach of the St. Michael's team was Scott McLellan. "Even as a young kid, Eric was completely focused on hockey," McLellan said. "I could blast him for mistakes like older players and he never sulked and was never intimidated."

JUNIOR HOCKEY

Canada's junior hockey leagues are big business. Teams from around the country draft the best young players each year. Junior-A is the top division, and is just a step below the NHL. Players drafted to Junior-A may have to leave home to play for their teams. High school kids often leave their families to play hockey in other towns.

The system has been successful at developing some of the world's greatest hockey players. A junior league team plays many more games per year than an American high school team. Players become local heroes who are seen on television and read about in newspapers. For most players, being uprooted is a small price to pay for a chance at fame or a job in the NHL.

In 1989, Eric was drafted by the Sault Ste. Marie (Soo Saint Marie) Greyhounds, a Junior-A team in the Ontario Hockey League (OHL). He was 16 years old, and was the first player chosen overall. Sault Ste. Marie is over 300 miles (483 km) from Toronto. Eric's parents wanted him to play closer to home, and that's when the controversy began.

Rather than accept the offer to play in Canada's Junior-A league, Eric's parents sent him to Detroit, Michigan. It was much closer to home, and Eric could live with friends of the family. His parents were trying to make sure Eric kept up with his school work. They enrolled him in an American high school, and he played hockey for a commercially sponsored amateur team in Detroit.

Hockey fans in Canada were not happy. The nation's best young prospect was playing in the United States. After seven months, the OHL made special arrangements for Eric to play closer to home.

*Eric Lindros on the
Canada Cup Team.*

*Eric Lindros (88) of the Canada Cup Team flies
past Patrick Dunn of the French Team.*

The league allowed Sault Ste. Marie to trade him to the Oshawa Generals. The Greyhounds received three players, three future draft picks and $80,000 for the rights to Eric. The Lindros family had won their battle with the junior leagues.

Eric made an immediate impact on the Generals. The team sold out every game Eric played in Oshawa's 4,200 seat arena. Unfortunately, his refusal to play for the Greyhounds had given him a bad reputation away from the home ice.

In Sault Ste. Marie, players wore black arm-bands to protest his selection to the All-Star team. Fans there thought Eric had insulted their community. They taunted him, bringing pacifiers to the games and calling him 'mommy's boy.'

In Eric's first season with the Generals, they won the 1990 Memorial Cup, Canada's junior hockey championship. In the 1990-91 season, he led the OHL in scoring with 71 goals and 78 assists in only 57 games! The Generals lost to the Greyhounds in the OHL playoffs amid more jeering from the fans.

CANADA CUP

In September 1991, the Canada Cup tournament was held for the fifth time in sixteen years. It is an international tournament which pits the best players from six hockey nations to determine a world champion. Participants in the 1991 competition came from Canada, Czechoslovakia, Finland, Sweden, the United States and the Soviet Union.

Eric was invited to try out for Team Canada. At 18 years old, 6-feet 5-inches (2 m) tall, and 224 pounds (102 kg), he was the only amateur player to make the squad. His teammates included NHL superstars Wayne Gretzky, Mark Messier, Paul Coffey and Brent Sutter. The competition was loaded with professional stars as well.

Eric played well in the tournament despite having to endure the second controversy of his young career. In June 1991, the Quebec Nordiques selected him as the first player taken in the NHL draft. Eric made it publicly clear that he would not sign a contract to play in Quebec. This time, he had outraged an entire province.

Quebec City, where the Nordiques play, is the capital of Quebec Province. Political debate over whether or not the French-speaking province should secede from the union of Canada was at a peak.

Eric Lindros (88) struggles with French goal keeper, J.M. Djian.

*The Canada Cup gave Eric
a chance to prove he was
ready for the NHL.*

Hockey fans in Quebec accused Eric of discrimination against their province.

Eric responded by saying he had nothing against the people of Quebec. He simply did not want to play for an organization which had been the worst team in the NHL for three years in a row. Some of the Canada Cup games were played in Quebec. When Team Canada arrived, Eric was again the target of fan abuse.

His first game with Team Canada was an exhibition against Team USA in Montreal, Quebec. The Montreal Forum was filled with 14,377 hostile fans who booed every time Eric stepped onto the ice. Eric scored two second-period goals and got an assist in the third period. When he was announced as the player of the game, he received an ovation as loud as the boos had been earlier.

The Canada Cup gave Eric a chance to prove he was ready for the NHL. He scored three goals and had two assists in eight tournament games. He skated on a power play unit which included Gretzky and Coffey. He teamed up with 'The Great One' on several occasions, scoring goals and bringing the crowds to their feet. Team Canada won the Cup, defeating Team USA in the finals. When it was over, Eric headed back to the junior leagues.

GO FOR THE GOLD!

Eric stuck to his word after the Canada Cup tournament, and did not sign a contract with the Nordiques. He kept himself busy during the 1991-92 season while waiting for Quebec to trade him to another NHL team.

After graduating from high school, Eric enrolled at Toronto's York University. He was still eligible to play junior hockey since he was not yet 20 years old. His hockey season was divided between three teams: the Oshawa Generals, Canada's National Junior team and the Canadian Olympic team.

Eric had led Canada to World Junior Hockey championships in the previous two seasons. The 1991-92 team finished sixth, and was subject to much criticism for their poor performance. The Olympics provided a chance for the Canadian amateurs to redeem themselves in international hockey.

The 1992 Olympic games were held in Albertville, France. Canada's greatest hockey players normally don't get a chance to compete in the games, since they are busy in the NHL. Eric's holdout provided him with the chance to represent his country.

Eric led Canada to the World Junior Hockey championships.

Canada's Olympic hockey team had not won a medal since they took home the bronze in 1968. With Eric leading the 1992 team, hopes were high that they could win the gold.

The team played an exhibition schedule to prepare for the trip to France. Games were scheduled against NHL teams including a game, which Eric sat out, against the Quebec Nordiques. His situation was a strange one. He was the star player for his country's team, but he was disliked by many fans because of his stalemate with the Nordiques.

Canada advanced to the medal round of the Olympic tournament with the best record in their pool. Other medal-round contenders included Team USA, Czechoslovakia and the Unified Team. The Unified Team represented countries which were formerly part of the Soviet Union.

Canada defeated the Czechs in their semifinal game. The Unified Team advanced to the final with a win over Team USA. In the gold medal match, the Unified Team proved too strong for the Canadian contingent, winning the game 3-1. Eric and his teammates took home silver medals.

FLYERS BY A THUMB

The 1992 NHL draft was held in June. Eric's holdout had reached one year. League regulations allow a team two years to sign their draft picks. Nordiques' management realized they needed to trade Eric, or risk losing his value entirely.

Marcel Aubut was the Nordiques' president and co-owner. He let it be known that Eric was available to any team that would offer a combination of players, future draft picks and cash. It was widely believed that Eric would be the next superstar of the league. With this in mind, the auction for Eric had begun.

Seven teams made offers to the Nordiques. Aubut accepted two. Two, however, was one too many! Eric had been traded to the Philadelphia Flyers and the New York Rangers at the same time.

Confusion reigned. The Flyers' president, Jay Snider, had offered Aubut a deal, sending six players, two draft picks, and $15 million to the Nordiques for the right to sign Eric. Aubut agreed to the deal by giving a thumbs up signal to Snider. Before finalizing the agreement, Snider wanted to O.K. the deal with Eric.

Snider talked to Eric on the telephone, and Eric agreed to become a Flyer. Meanwhile, the Rangers offered Aubut a sweeter deal which included $20 million. Aubut told the Rangers the deal was theirs.

When Snider found out his deal had been thrown out, he went straight to league president, John Ziegler, to cry foul. The league hired lawyer Larry Bertuzzi to decide which team would get Eric.

Bertuzzi heard testimony from all parties involved. He determined Eric was a member of the Philadelphia Flyers. The deciding factor was Aubut's thumb.

NEW BULLY IN TOWN

The Flyers made Eric the highest-paid player in NHL history. They had given up a lot of money and talent to bring him to town. The team had finished in last place the previous season. They were not a good team, but they were banking on Eric to bring back the glory days of the "Broad Street Bullies."

Eric's size and strength made him perfect for the part. Not many hockey players measure up to Eric's 6-foot, 5-inch (2 m), 235 pound (107 km) frame. When he's not blazing up ice with the puck, he's blistering opponents with body checks. He is not unfamiliar with the penalty box.

*Philadelphia Flyers Eric Lindros (left) shoves past Quebec Nordiques
Mikhail Tatarinov, 1992.*

Hockey fans and the media anticipated Eric's NHL arrival with great enthusiasm. He was called "the most ballyhooed rookie in the history of professional sports," by ESPN's executive editor, John Walsh. The Flyers opened the season against the defending Stanley Cup Champion Pittsburgh Penguins on national cable television in the United States.

Eric was under enormous pressure to perform. He was called everything from "Gretzky with muscles," to the "savior of professional hockey." With all of this attention, he scored four goals and had three assists in his first seven NHL games.

Eric finished the 1992-93 season with 41 goals in 61 games. He missed two months of the season because of a knee injury. The next season, Eric scored 44 goals while missing another 19 games due to an injured knee. The Flyers missed the playoffs both years.

LEGION OF DOOM

The 1994-95 NHL season was cut short by a labor dispute between players and owners. When the season finally got started, the Flyers organization had made some important changes.

Bobby Clarke, a star player for Philadelphia in the 1970s, was the new team president and general manager. He hired Terry Murray as the new head coach. Eric became team captain at 21 years old, and in only his third professional season.

In February, the Flyers traded high-scoring winger Mark Recchi to the Montreal Canadians for defenseman Eric Desjardins, and wingers John LeClair and Gilbert Dionne. The trade worked out well for the Flyers. Desjardins strengthened the defense, and LeClair joined Eric and Mikael Renberg to form the most dominating line in the league.

The new line-mates became known as the "Legion of Doom." They combined to score 79 goals in their 35 games together. The Flyers were 23-8-4 in games after the Legion was formed. Philadelphia finished the season with a record of 28-16-4, to win the Atlantic Division and advance to the playoffs.

Eric's 70 points, on 29 goals and 41 assists, tied Pittsburgh's Jaromir Jagr for the league lead. Jagr was awarded the scoring title based on a tie-breaker of most goals. Eric was named the Hart Memorial Trophy winner as the NHL's Most Valuable Player.

The Flyers defeated the Buffalo Sabres and New York Rangers in the first two rounds of the playoffs. They were knocked out by the New Jersey Devils in a six game Conference Final. The Devils won the 1995 Stanley Cup with a four game sweep over the Detroit Red Wings.

Eric became team captain at 21 years old, and in only his third professional season.

JUST A KID

Eric Lindros is just beginning what promises to be an excellent professional career. At 22 years old, he became the youngest player since Gretzky to win the MVP award in the NHL. He has put controversy behind him to become the superstar player everyone expected him to be.

Eric is a leader. He is captain of his team, and has been the master of his own destiny. He has been filling hockey arenas since he was 16 years old. Twice, he has fought for and won the right to play hockey where he wants.

Eric has been stirring up hockey's old established ways for a long time. Now hockey is looking for Eric to lead the way into the next century.   Philadelphia Flyer fans are waiting for Eric to bring the Stanley Cup back to Broad Street. It's only a matter of time.

*Eric Lindros was named the Hart Memorial Trophy winner
as the NHL's Most Valuable Player.*

GLOSSARY

Accountant: One that keeps, audits, and inspects the financial records for an individual or business.

Amateur: A person who performs without being paid.

Assist: A pass in hockey that enables a teammate to score.

Canada Cup: An international hockey tournament for the best players in the world, hosted by Canada on an irregular basis.

Captain: The designated leader of a team or crew in sports.

Center: The position in hockey reserved for the best puck-handlers and fastest skaters, positioned between the two wingers. The center also handles all face-offs.

Check: The act of blocking or impeding an opponent in control of the puck in ice hockey, either with one's body or one's stick.

Contract: A written agreement a player signs when they are hired by a professional team.

Controversy: A dispute, especially a public one, between sides holding opposing views.

Defenseman: A position in hockey reserved for players who skate backwards well and are adept at checking. The defensemen help the goalie by obstructing the progress of the opposition.

Destiny: The inevitable or necessary fate to which a particular person or thing is destined; one's lot.

Discrimination: To make distinctions on the basis of class or category without regard to individual merit; show preference or prejudice.

Draft: A system in which new players are distributed to professional sports teams.

Minor leagues: A system of professional hockey leagues at levels below the NHL.

National Hockey League (NHL): An organization of professional hockey teams in North America.

Olympics: A group of modern international athletic contests held every four years in a different city.

Ontario Hockey League (OHL): An organization of amateur hockey teams for players under the age of 20 in the province of Ontario, Canada.

Prospect: A player who is expected to succeed at the next level.

Province: A territory governed as an administrative or political unit of a country or an empire.

Stanley Cup: The large silver trophy given each year to the NHL champions. The names of the winning players are engraved on the side of the trophy each year.

Testimony: A declaration by a witness under oath offered in a legal case or deliberative hearing.

Winger: A position in hockey reserved for fast skaters and accurate shooters. In normal situations, there are two wingers on the ice for each team, the left wing and right wing positions.

Index